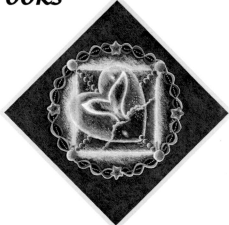

Expressions
of
Spirit

Barbara Alana Brooks

Published by
barbsartwork.com

Available from Amazon.com and other retail outlets.

ISBN-13: 978-0692417140
ISBN-10: 0692417141

~DEDICATION~

With love and gratitude to my mother and
nurturing mothers everywhere.

My mother: Ruth Baumann Jacobson (1922)
As a child, she loved being a ballerina,
As an adult, she loved art and painting.

~FORWARD~

"The mandala is an archetypal image whose occurrence is attested throughout the ages. It signifies the wholeness of the self. The circular image represents the wholeness of the psychic ground or, to put it in mythic terms, the divinity incarnate in man." Carl Jung, Memories, Dreams, Reflections, N.Y., Random House, 1963, p. 334.

I look at each of Barbara's mandalas as prayers. Any one of these beautifully rendered works could be an object of focus for a meditation. For example, the mandala of Courage invites us to move to our own center and inquire about what courage means in our own life. When have we felt courageous? And when have we felt lacking in courage? Going more deeply than demonstrations of outer courage, what about the inner courage to face our own shadows or hidden fears? Why did Barbara select a horse to be at the Center of the mandala, with an overlay of a triangle and yet another miniature mandala at the very heart of the Universe represented by the outer rim of the entire circle? How does all this mirror our inner Universe? Personally, I'm so inspired by Barbara's mandalas, that I intend to create my own as a depiction of the Divinity within my own Soul. This is how Carl Jung drew many of his interpretations of his dreams, his way of revelation of meaning in his life and of others. Barbara's mandalas are an invitation to all of us to create our own mandalas in order to relax deeply into the Centers of our True Selves.

Caroline Blakemore, Spiritual Director, artist and author

List of Mandalas

Creative Heart
Respect
Focus
Expansion
Light
Dream Walker
Angel of Joy
Well-Being
Unconditional Love
Relationship
Beauty Within
Divine Human Blueprint
Direction
Courage
Passion
Enthusiasm
Nature's Symphony
Life
Infinity
Nurturing
Tenderness
Transformation
Pink Harmony
Love's Magic
Connection
Possibilities
New Life
Spirit of America

~INTRODUCTION~

For thousands of years, people from all cultures and spiritual traditions created circular designs referred to as mandalas for healing and meditation. These images represent wholeness, unity and infinity. Mandala art is known for its transformational qualities.

Tibetan monks drew mandalas and Navajo Native Americans created medicine wheels and round sand paintings. The Pennsylvania Dutch created colorful circular symbols on their barns for protection and good luck. Look to nature and notice that flowers are mandalas, our eyes are mandalas and a cut tree trunk is a mandala.

As you look at these designs, notice which ones attract you. Some people are drawn to the art and others to the words that accompany each design. Focus your attention on the ones that pull you in because hidden in the design might be a message of healing and transformation.

Creative Heart

In the soul of every human being beats the creative heart.
We came to this fertile physical environment
to be creators in our own unique way.

Respect

Give thanks to all those in your life
who inspire joy and love in your heart.

Focus

As a conscious creator of your life, deliberately
focus your attention on solutions
and what you want rather than problems.

Expansion

In an eternally expanding universe, we are the microcosm
of the macrocosm constantly inspired to explore
and experience new stimulation, excitement and passion.

Light

Let your inner radiance sparkle.

Dream Walker

Our dreams bring us valuable messages from our soul.

Angel of Joy

There is always so much for which to be happy and grateful.

Well-Being

Our natural state as human beings is health, happiness and well-being.

23

Unconditional Love

This mandala was created for my beloved dog, Cookie, who made her transition in 2000. I was unaware while creating it that a paw print was unfolding in the picture.

25

Relationship

All our interactions with each other, the animals, and the environment,
reflect back to us who we are and who we are becoming.

(The six-pointed star is also an ancient Egyptian symbol for wholeness.)

Beauty Within

Behold your own magnificence and listen to your inner voice.

Divine Human Blueprint

Within each of us is a master plan for perfect health and well-being.

Direction

Within each of us is an inner compass called our emotion.
We become empowered creators of our life experience
when we choose thoughts that feel good.

33

Courage

Be adventuresome and follow your passion.

Passion

Say yes to the delicious, juicy experiences of life.

37

Enthusiasm

Find exhilaration and fun in each day.
Relax and play more.

Nature's Symphony

In the heart of nature exists perfect harmony that is available to us through our intention and awareness.

Life

The power of creation surges from the volcanoes and the sea.
That energy exists in each of us.

*(Inspired from swimming with the wild dolphins
off the Big Island of Hawaii.)*

43

Infinity

The dolphins are reminding us that our lives
are eternal and multi-dimensional.

Nurturing

Like a mother and her baby, we, too, must nourish ourselves
with love, compassion and self acceptance.

*(Inspired by swimming with the humpback whales on
The Silver Bank off the Dominican Republic.)*

Tenderness

Within the depths of ourselves is unconditional self love.

Transformation

Just as the caterpillar becomes a butterfly, we can transform
ourselves through our desire and intention.

Pink Harmony

The cells in my body know how to achieve harmony.
I can trust my body.

(Created to spread awareness about breast cancer in conjunction
with the Komen Portland Race for the Cure.
This picture was used in a traveling national exhibit.)

"Tranformation"

Love's Magic

Deep love for another has the power to transform your life.

Connection

Inspired in Peru by the rich history of the Inca civilization
and their amazing connection to Pacamama or Mother Earth.

Possibilities

Living in the physical dimension of contrasting experiences evokes
desire and infinite choices. That desire summons the life force
and fuels new creations.

New Life

Each generation of every species brings a sparkle of freshness, excitement and anticipation for the future.

Spirit of America

Our forefathers saw adversity as an opportunity.
Out of chaos comes clarity.

(Created after September 11, 2001)

A Note from the Artist:

When I drew my first mandala, I felt an immediate attraction to this art form. I couldn't stop drawing them because I felt a sense of peace and balance from the symmetry and geometric shapes. My art is inspired by the beauty and patterns in the physical world as well as my internal vision. A personal fascination with these symbols is their ability to calm the inner and outer chaos experienced by the majority of people in our crazy, busy world including myself. I make a conscious effort to create art in an environment of love and harmony. When you gaze at a design, allow yourself to relax into a place of stillness and tranquility. Be present with the mandala.

Many of my designs are associated with an event or experience in my life. I swam with the wild spinner dolphins near the Big Island in Hawaii resulting in Life, Enthusiasm, Infinity and Nature's Symphony. This experience led to a trip to the Dominican Republic where I lived on a boat for a week and swam with the humpback whales on the Silver Bank. The whales migrate there each winter to mate and have their babies inspiring the design of Nurturing and Tenderness. Visiting the sacred site of Machu Piechu in Peru stimulated the mandala Connection.

All of my mandalas are hand drawn using pencil, pastel and acrylic paint. When I draw a new design, I set an intention to connect with the sacred energies of the universe and bring forth a symbol that will inspire me as well as anyone who may see it. I feel honored to share these energies that have touched my own heart and perhaps will affect yours as well.

Barbara Alana Brooks